"BE·MUCH OCCUPIED —WITH— JESUS"

SEA HARP PRESS

SPURGEON QUOTES

|||||||||||||||||||||||||||||||||||||||||||||||||||||||||||||||||||||||||||||||||

100 Words on Encountering Jesus
By the "Prince of Preachers"

Spurgeon Quotes by Charles H. Spurgeon

This edition copyright © 2022—Sea Harp
An imprint of Nori Media Group
P.O. Box 310, Shippensburg, PA 17257-0310
"Be Much Occupied with Jesus"

Cover design and interior page design copyright 2022.

All rights reserved.

Cover design by Christian Rafetto

Foreword by Eugene Luning

All rights reserved. This book is protected by the copyright laws of the United States of America. This book may not be copied or reprinted for commercial gain or profit. The use of short quotations or occasional page copying for personal or group study is permitted and encouraged. Permission will be granted upon request.

This book and all other Sea Harp books are available at Christian bookstores and distributors worldwide.

For more information on foreign distributors, call 717-532-3040.

Reach us on the Internet: www.seaharp.com

ISBN 13 TP: 978-0-7684-7454-1

ISBN 13 eBook: 978-0-7684-7455-8

For Worldwide Distribution.

1 2 3 4 5 6 7 8 / 26 25 24 23 22

FOREWORD

Charles H. Spurgeon, for all his life's accomplishments—his books, his many famous sermon series, his building projects, his God-given affability, his evangelistic successes, his worldwide renown, his ongoing "fame" in the collective Christian consciousness—was, fundamentally, a lover of God. His books and messages are really nothing but the overflow of an abiding, daily experience of the indwelling life of Jesus, the voice of the Spirit, the love of the Father.

Our goal in this short work is to give a "sampler" of the sorts of glorious things he so often said and wrote, to invite your heart nearer to God through the words of one who really knew Him. Oftentimes, the most joyous experience of Spurgeon is in his peculiar, sparkling turns of phrase; in the way he weaves a truth into a single sentence or short paragraph.

We trust that by your reading these short, varied fragments we might entice your later reading in long form!

Thank you for being part of the Sea Harp Family!

❝

I cannot know Jesus through another person's acquaintance with him. No, I must know him *myself*; I must know him on my own account.

CHARLES H. SPURGEON

From the first moment of your spiritual life until you are ushered into glory, the language of Christ to you will be, "*Come, come* unto me."

All earthly suns have their spots: the fair world itself hath its wilderness; we cannot love the whole of the most lovely thing; but Christ Jesus is gold without alloy—light without darkness—glory without cloud—"Yea, he is *altogether* lovely."

"

From the night of natural depravity, of ignorance, of doubt, of despair, of sin, of dread, Jesus has come to set us free; and all believers shall know that he no more comes in vain than the sun rises and fails to scatter his heat and light.

However difficult and painful thy road, it is marked by the footsteps of thy Saviour; and even when thou reachest the dark valley of the shadow of death, and the deep waters of the swelling Jordan, thou wilt find his footprints there.

CHARLES H. SPURGEON

> What wouldst thou do at night, when thou comest home jaded and weary, if there were no door of fellowship between thee and Christ? Blessed be his name, he will not suffer us to try our lot without him, for Jesus never forsakes his own.

> In Christ Jesus the pure in heart behold the Father. We see him, his truth, his love, his purpose, his sovereignty, his covenant character, yea, we see himself in Christ.

CHARLES H. SPURGEON

God is nigh to forgive, to bless, to comfort, to help, to quicken, to deliver. Let it be the main point with us to get near to God. This done, all is done.

> Jesus is to me all grace and no wrath, all truth and no falsehood: and of truth and grace he is *full*, infinitely full.

CHARLES H. SPURGEON

You may look, and study, and weigh, but Jesus is a greater Saviour than you think him to be when your thoughts are at the greatest. My Lord is more ready to pardon than you to sin, more able to forgive than you to transgress. My Master is more willing to supply your wants than you are to confess them. Never tolerate low thoughts of my Lord Jesus.

> ...our Master knows no limit of power or boundary of mission. He is so prolific of grace, that like the sun which shines as it rolls onward in its orbit, his path is radiant with lovingkindness.

CHARLES H. SPURGEON

> That hand which multiplied the loaves, which saved sinking Peter, which upholds afflicted saints, which crowns believers, that same hand will touch every seeking sinner, and in a moment make him clean. The love of Jesus is the source of salvation.

> The more you know about Christ the less will you be satisfied with superficial views of him; and the more deeply you study his transactions in the eternal covenant, his engagements on your behalf as the eternal Surety, and the fulness of his grace which shines in all his offices, the more truly will you see the King in his beauty. Be much in such outlooks.

CHARLES H. SPURGEON

>

...what our Lord was he is, and what he was to those with whom he lived on earth, he will be to all his beloved so long as the moon endureth.

> It is no wonder that the Lord's people should be satisfied with the goodness of their Lord. Here is goodness without mixture, bounty without stint, mercy without chiding, love without change, favor without reserve. If God's goodness does not satisfy us, what will?

CHARLES H. SPURGEON

There is such a fulness in Christ that he alone is the believer's all. The true saint is so completely satisfied with the all-sufficiency of Jesus that he thirsts no more—except it be for deeper draughts of the living fountain.

> Lord Jesus, I have found thee;
> be found of me to an unutterable
> degree of joyous satisfaction.

CHARLES H. SPURGEON

> ...a look at the Great Saviour will heal you of [all] diseases, and make you live in holiness and communion with God. Look and live.

> Let us sit at the feet of Jesus, and by earnest prayer call in his blessed aid that our dull wits may grow brighter, and our feeble understandings may receive heavenly things.

CHARLES H. SPURGEON

> Lord, grant thine unworthy one his desire, for I am thine, and thou hast bought me with thy blood. Thou hast opened mine eye to see thee, and the sight has saved me. Lord, open thou mine ear. I have read thy heart, now let me hear thy lips.

Christians may differ on a variety of points, but they have all one spiritual appetite; and if we cannot all *feel* alike, we can all *feed* alike on the bread of life sent down from heaven.

CHARLES H. SPURGEON

O believer, God's acceptance of Christ is thine acceptance; for knowest thou not that the love which the Father set on a perfect Christ, he sets on thee *now*? For all that Christ did is thine.

> We must receive the truths which Jesus taught, the precepts which he issued, and the movements of his Spirit within us; or we shall have no power at the mercy-seat.

CHARLES H. SPURGEON

> To live by faith is a far surer and happier thing than to live by feelings or by works. The branch, by living in the vine, lives a better life than it would live by itself, even if it were possible for it to live at all apart from the stem. To live by clinging to Jesus, by deriving all from him, is a sweet and sacred thing.

> Come, weary one, use thy Lord's words as thy pillows. Lie down in peace. Dream only of him. Jesus is thy ladder of light.

CHARLES H. SPURGEON

"

The moment a sinner trusts
Jesus he is fully forgiven.

> Let us be of good cheer, Christ has borne the load before us, and the blood-stained footsteps of the King of glory may be seen along the road which we traverse at this hour.

CHARLES H. SPURGEON

His love was indeed stronger than the most terrible death, for it endured the trial of the cross triumphantly. It was a lingering death, but love survived the torment; a shameful death, but love despised the shame....

The Christian is perfectly saved *in God's purpose*; God has ordained him unto salvation, and that purpose is complete... "It is finished."

CHARLES H. SPURGEON

Jesus has emptied the quivers of hell, has quenched every fiery dart, and broken off the head of every arrow of wrath; the ground is strewn with the splinters and relics of the weapons of hell's warfare....

> The Great Lord will not remember our sins so as to punish them, or so as to love us one atom the less because of them. As a debt when paid ceases to be a debt, even so doth the Lord make a complete obliteration of the iniquity of his people.

CHARLES H. SPURGEON

> Jesus must clothe his people in his own garments, or he cannot admit them into his palace of glory; and he must wash them in his own blood, or else they will be too defiled for the embrace of his fellowship.

> He who fights with the precious blood of Jesus, fights with a weapon which cannot know defeat. The blood of Jesus! sin dies at its presence, death ceases to be death: heaven's gates are opened. The blood of Jesus! we shall march on, conquering and to conquer, so long as we can trust its power!

CHARLES H. SPURGEON

> To know a crucified Saviour as having crucified all my sins, is a high degree of knowledge; but to know a risen Saviour as having justified me, and to realize that he has bestowed upon me new life, having given me to be a new creature through his own newness of life, this is a noble style of experience....

> He is risen, I am risen in him, why then should I cleave unto the dust? From lower loves, desires, pursuits, and aspirations, I would rise towards him. He calls me by the sweet title of "My love...."

CHARLES H. SPURGEON

> If he had not loved me with a love as deep as hell, and as strong as death, he would have turned from me long ago. Oh, joy above all joys, to know that I am his everlasting and inalienable inheritance, given to him by his Father or ever the earth was!

"

What a joy to belong to a kingdom in which everything is being made new by the power of its King! We are not dying out: we are hastening on to a more glorious life.

CHARLES H. SPURGEON

> Lord Jesus, turn in with me and be my guest; and then walk out with me, and cause my heart to burn while you speak with me by the way.

Jesus is the keeper of the gates of paradise and before every believing soul he setteth an open door, which no man or devil shall be able to close against it. What joy it will be to find that faith in him is the golden key to the everlasting doors.

CHARLES H. SPURGEON

> All the love and the acceptance which perfect obedience could have obtained of God, belong to thee, because Christ was perfectly obedient on thy behalf, and hath imputed all his merits to thy account, that thou mightst be exceeding rich through him, who for thy sake became exceeding poor.

Christ at the right hand of God hath all power in heaven and in earth. Who shall fight against the people who have such power vested in their Captain? O my soul, what can destroy thee if Omnipotence be thy helper?

His high estate is as much at our service as was his condition of abasement. He who gave himself for us in the depths of woe and death, doth not withdraw the grant now that he is enthroned in the highest heavens.

> Jesus has made the life of his people as eternal as his own. How can they die as long as he lives, seeing they are one with him?

CHARLES H. SPURGEON

Those eyes which once wept for us, are now viewing us with pleasure. Yes, he looks upon those who are looking unto him. Our eyes meet! What a joy is this!

Christ is the solace of our life. All our true joys come from him; and in times of trouble, his presence is our consolation. There is nothing worth living for but him; and his lovingkindness is better than life!

My soul, thou hast a friend well fitted to be thine advocate, he cannot but succeed; leave thyself entirely in his hands.

> In him a stairway of light now furnishes a clear passage to the throne of the Most High. Let us use it, and send up by it the messengers of our prayers.

CHARLES H. SPURGEON

"*I am the Lord, I change not.*" The stability which the anchor gives the ship when it has at last obtained a hold-fast, is like that which the Christian's hope affords him when it fixes itself upon this glorious truth.

> God himself, in Christ Jesus,
> is the sanctuary of mercy.

CHARLES H. SPURGEON

It will be a joy to Jesus to give you liberty. It will give him as great a pleasure to loose you as it will be a pleasure to you to be loosed.

> When Jesus receives sinners, he has not some out-of-doors reception place, no casual ward where he charitably entertains them as men do passing beggars, but he opens the golden gates of his royal heart, and receives the sinner right into himself....

CHARLES H. SPURGEON

" Our God ignores our sin now that the sacrifice of Jesus has ratified the covenant. We may rejoice in him without fear that he will be provoked to anger against us because of our iniquities. See! He puts us among the children; he accepts us as righteous; he takes delight in us as if we were perfectly holy.

…if we fear God, we have nothing else to fear; if we cry to the Lord, our salvation is certain.

>

Among the lost souls in hell there is not one that can say, "I went to Jesus, and he refused me." It is not possible that you or I should be the first to whom Jesus shall break his word. Let us not entertain so dark a suspicion.

> By all the memories of the Lord's former lovingkindnesses let us rest assured that he will not forsake us. He who has gone so far as to make us his people, will not undo the creation of his grace.

— CHARLES H. SPURGEON

When Jesus comes into the heart, he issues a general licence to be glad in the Lord. No chains are worn in the court of King Jesus. Our admission into full privileges may be gradual, but it is sure.

We are sure that the Lord will continue his mercies to his own people. He does not give and take. What he has granted us is the token of much more.

> Come to Jesus, by quitting every other hope, by thinking of him, believing God's testimony about him, and trusting everything with him. If you thus come to him, the rest which he will give you will be deep, safe, holy, and everlasting. He gives a rest which develops into heaven, and he gives it this day to all who come to him.

> The breadth of his tender love is such that you may resort to him in all matters; for in all your afflictions he is afflicted, and like as a father pitieth his children, so doth he pity you. The meanest interests of all his saints are all borne upon the broad bosom of the Son of God. Oh, what a heart is his!

What can the Lord deny us after giving us Jesus? If we need all things in Heaven and earth, he will grant them to us: for if there had been a limit anywhere, he would have kept back his own Son.

>

If God cares for you, why need you care too? Can you trust him for your soul, and not for your body? He has never refused to bear your burdens, he has never fainted under their weight.

CHARLES H. SPURGEON

> The Lord is concerned about everything that concerns me. All that is now good, but not perfect, the Lord will watch over, and preserve, and carry out to completion. This is a great comfort.

When we pray aright we speak into the ear of God. Our gracious Mediator presents our petitions at once, and the great Father hears them and smiles upon them. Grand praying this!

> Tell the Lord all about thy grief, and leave it with him. Don't cast your burden down, and then take it up again; but roll it on the Lord, and leave it there.

" It is a Christian's duty to force his way into the inner circle of saintship; and if these saints [from the Bible] were superior to us in their attainments, as they certainly were, let us follow them; let us emulate their ardour and holiness. We have the same light that they had, the same grace is accessible to us....

CHARLES H. SPURGEON

Whatever thou mayest think of thyself, if Christ be great to thee, thou shalt be with him ere long.

> All earthly bliss is of the earth earthy, but the comforts of Christ's presence are like himself, heavenly. We can review our communion with Jesus, and find no regrets of emptiness therein; there are no dregs in this wine, no dead flies in this ointment. The joy of the Lord is solid and enduring.

CHARLES H. SPURGEON

> To embrace our Lord Jesus, to dwell in his love, and be fully assured of union with him—this is all in all.

He is our refuge, let us hide in him; he is our strength, let us array ourselves with him; he is our help, let us lean upon him; he is our very present help, let us repose in him now. We need not have a moment's care, or an instant's fear.

CHARLES H. SPURGEON

> Unless the Eternal One himself can undergo change, his ways, which are himself in action, must remain forever the same. Is he eternally just, gracious, faithful, wise, tender?—then his ways must ever be distinguished for the same excellences.

We share the honour of Christ, and compared with this, earthly splendours are not worth a thought. Communion with Jesus is a richer gem than ever glittered in imperial diadem. Union with the Lord is a coronet of beauty outshining all the blaze of imperial pomp.

CHARLES H. SPURGEON

God upholds me. God abides with me. Whom shall I fear?

> Happy are those who place their hand in that of the great Guide, and leave their way and themselves entirely with him. He will bring them all the way....

CHARLES H. SPURGEON

Faith sees God with a transforming look. The heart receives the image of Jesus into its own depths, till the character of Jesus is imprinted on the soul. This is satisfaction.

> The golden streets of paradise, the pearly gates, the river of life, the transcendent bliss, and the unutterable glory, are, by our blessed Lord, made over to us for our everlasting possession. All that he has he shares with his people.

CHARLES H. SPURGEON

> When you enter heaven you shall find him there bearing the dew of his youth; and through eternity the Lord Jesus shall still remain the perennial spring of joy, and life, and glory to his people. Living waters may you draw from this sacred well! Jesus always was, he always is, he always shall be.

Our Lord Jesus is ever giving, and does not for a solitary instant withdraw his hand. As long as there is a vessel of grace not yet full to the brim, the oil shall not be stayed.

CHARLES H. SPURGEON

The Holy Ghost is no temporary gift, he abides with the saints. We have but to seek him aright, and he will be found of us.

> Let us seek the illumination of the Spirit; not to gratify our curiosity, nor even to bring us personal comfort, so much as to glorify the Lord Jesus. Oh, to have worthy ideas of him!

CHARLES H. SPURGEON

> I am only asking what he delights to give. I am sure that he will condescend to have fellowship with me, for he has given me his Holy Spirit to abide with me forever.

> ...see his kindness, he has built his house next door to ours, nay, more, he takes lodging with us, and tabernacles in poor humble hearts, that so he may have perpetual interconnection with us. O how foolish must we be, if we do not live in habitual communion with him.

CHARLES H. SPURGEON

> There is a life within us which is not capable of being divided from God: yea, and the Holy Spirit dwells within us, and how then can we die? Jesus, Himself, is our life, and therefore there is no dying for us, for he cannot die again.

> Come, my heart, cheer up! In a little while I shall be as glad as I am now gloomy. Jesus tells me that by a heavenly alchemy my sorrow shall be turned into joy. I do not see how it is to be, but I believe it, and I begin to sing by way of anticipation.

CHARLES H. SPURGEON

If the Holy Spirit be indeed so mighty, let us attempt nothing without him; let us begin no project, and carry on no enterprise, and conclude no transaction, without imploring his blessing.

> Oh, how precious is Christ! How can it be that I have thought so little of him? How is it I can go abroad for joy or comfort when he is so full, so rich, so satisfying?

CHARLES H. SPURGEON

> Seek with your whole soul, first and foremost, the kingdom of God, as the place of your citizenship, and his righteousness as the character of your life. As for the rest, it will come from the Lord himself without your being anxious concerning it.

> If you would have Christ with you, seek him boldly. Let nothing hold you back. Defy the world. Press on where others flee.

CHARLES H. SPURGEON

> Exiles though we be, we rejoice in our King; yea, in him we exceedingly rejoice, while in his name we set up our banners.

> He has emptied all his estate into the coffers of the Church, and hath all things common with his redeemed. There is not one room in his house the key of which he will withhold from his people. He gives them full liberty to take all that he hath to be their own....

CHARLES H. SPURGEON

Blessed be the Lord, I am no stranger to him. I have tried him, and proved him, and known him, and, therefore, do I trust him.

Let your first care be to glorify God to the utmost of your power where you are. Fill your present sphere to his praise, and if he needs you in another he will show it you.

CHARLES H. SPURGEON

The Lord our God condescends to serve us as guide. He knows the way, and will pilot us along it till we reach our journey's end in peace. Surely we do not desire more infallible direction.

> We should pant after love to Christ of a most abiding character, not a love that flames up and then dies out into the darkness of a few embers, but a constant flame, fed by sacred fuel, like the fire upon the altar which never went out. This cannot be accomplished except by faith.

CHARLES H. SPURGEON

The sight of our glorious Well-beloved will justify the most enthusiastic attachment to him. None will blame the martyrs for dying for him.

> Keep back no part of the precious truth, but speak what you know, and testify what you have seen. Let not the toil or darkness, or possible unbelief of your friends, weigh one moment in the scale. Up, and be marching to the place of duty, and there tell what great things God has shown to your soul.

CHARLES H. SPURGEON

> Cheerful holiness is the most forcible of sermons, but the Lord must give it you. Seek it this morning before you go into the world.

> If I imitate Jesus I shall have his company: if I am like him I shall be with him.

We do not need glory yet, and we are not yet fit for it; but we shall have it in due order. After we have eaten the bread of grace, we shall drink the wine of glory. We must go through the holy—which is grace, to the holiest of all—which is glory.

> To be for ever with the Lord is my idea of Heaven at its best. Not the harps of gold, nor the crowns unfading, nor the light unclouded, is glory to me; but Jesus, Jesus himself, and myself for ever with him in nearest and dearest fellowship.

CHARLES H. SPURGEON

O Lord, come quickly! There is no life in this earthly existence if thou be gone. We sigh for the return of thy sweet smile.

INDEX OF SOURCES

By Reading

pg 7. *Morning & Evening*	pg 21. *Faith's Checkbook*
pg 8. *Morning & Evening*	pg 22. *Morning & Evening*
pg 9. *Morning & Evening*	pg 23. *Faith's Checkbook*
pg 10. *Faith's Checkbook*	pg 24. *Faith's Checkbook*
pg 11. *Morning & Evening*	pg 25. *Morning & Evening*
pg 12. *Morning & Evening*	pg 26. *Morning & Evening*
pg 13. *Faith's Checkbook*	pg 27. *Morning & Evening*
pg 14. *Faith's Checkbook*	pg 28. *Morning & Evening*
pg 15. *Morning & Evening*	pg 29. *Faith's Checkbook*
pg 16. *Morning & Evening*	pg 30. *Faith's Checkbook*
pg 17. *Morning & Evening*	pg 31. *Faith's Checkbook*
pg 18. *Morning & Evening*	pg 32. *Morning & Evening*
pg 19. *Morning & Evening*	pg 33. *Morning & Evening*
pg 20. *Faith's Checkbook*	pg 34. *Morning & Evening*

pg 35. *Morning & Evening*	pg 53. *Faith's Checkbook*
pg 36. *Morning & Evening*	pg 54. *Morning & Evening*
pg 37. *Faith's Checkbook*	pg 55. *Faith's Checkbook*
pg 38. *Morning & Evening*	pg 56. *Faith's Checkbook*
pg 39. *Morning & Evening*	pg 57. *Morning & Evening*
pg 40. *Morning & Evening*	pg 58. *Faith's Checkbook*
pg 41. *Morning & Evening*	pg 59. *Faith's Checkbook*
pg 42. *Morning & Evening*	pg 60. *Faith's Checkbook*
pg 43. *Faith's Checkbook*	pg 61. *Faith's Checkbook*
pg 44. *Faith's Checkbook*	pg 62. *Morning & Evening*
pg 45. *Morning & Evening*	pg 63. *Faith's Checkbook*
pg 46. *Morning & Evening*	pg 64. *Faith's Checkbook*
pg 47. *Morning & Evening*	pg 65. *Morning & Evening*
pg 48. *Morning & Evening*	pg 66. *Faith's Checkbook*
pg 49. *Faith's Checkbook*	pg 67. *Morning & Evening*
pg 50. *Faith's Checkbook*	pg 68. *Faith's Checkbook*
pg 51. *Morning & Evening*	pg 69. *Faith's Checkbook*
pg 52. *Morning & Evening*	pg 70. *Faith's Checkbook*

pg 71. *Morning & Evening*	pg 89. *Faith's Checkbook*
pg 72. *Morning & Evening*	pg 90. *Morning & Evening*
pg 73. *Morning & Evening*	pg 91. *Morning & Evening*
pg 74. *Morning & Evening*	pg 92. *Faith's Checkbook*
pg 75. *Faith's Checkbook*	pg 93. *Morning & Evening*
pg 76. *Morning & Evening*	pg 94. *Morning & Evening*
pg 77. *Morning & Evening*	pg 95. *Morning & Evening*
pg 78. *Faith's Checkbook*	pg 96. *Faith's Checkbook*
pg 79. *Faith's Checkbook*	pg 97. *Morning & Evening*
pg 80. *Faith's Checkbook*	pg 98. *Faith's Checkbook*
pg 81. *Morning & Evening*	pg 99. *Morning & Evening*
pg 82. *Morning & Evening*	pg 100. *Faith's Checkbook*
pg 83. *Morning & Evening*	pg 101. *Morning & Evening*
pg 84. *Morning & Evening*	pg 102. *Morning & Evening*
pg 85. *Faith's Checkbook*	pg 103. *Faith's Checkbook*
pg 86. *Morning & Evening*	pg 104. *Faith's Checkbook*
pg 87. *Morning & Evening*	pg 105. *Faith's Checkbook*
pg 88. *Faith's Checkbook*	pg 106. *Faith's Checkbook*

ABOUT THE AUTHOR

Charles Haddon Spurgeon (1834-1892) was a British preacher, pastor, author, and theologian. A relentless disciple of Jesus, he was famed for his oratory and profound way with words; his sermons and books are a delight to both intellectuals and the average layperson. His passion for the Word of God and his inimitable style of leading his reader directly into the presence of each member of the Trinity have long been treasured by churchpeople all over the world. His own devotion to Jesus led him courageously through a full, and at times difficult, life; he stands today as one of the great saints of the last many centuries.

ABOUT
SEA HARP PRESS

Sea Harp is a specialty press with one overarching aim: in the words of Andrew Murray, to "be much occupied with Jesus, and believe much in Him, as the True Vine." Our mission is twofold: to reinvigorate the Church's reading of the best of the past, and to bring out fresh editions of both today's and tomorrow's classics — all for the purpose of personal encounter with Jesus Himself.

For every piece of media we consider publishing, we ask two fundamental questions:

- Is this work entirely about the person of Jesus of Nazareth?
- Would the Early Church have thought this work worthy of sharing?

We take our name from the original Hebrew word for the Sea of Galilee—*Kinneret*: כִּנֶּרֶת: meaning "harp"—which was given because of the harp-like shape of the shoreline around which Jesus ministered. It was, in less words, a place known as the Harp-Sea.

Thank you for joining us as we walk the Way with that most wonderful Man of Galilee.

the
SEA *of*
GALILEE

WWW.SEAHARP.COM

www.ingramcontent.com/pod-product-compliance
Lightning Source LLC
Chambersburg PA
CBHW031451040426
42444CB00007B/1062